PAIN PUSHED ME INTO PURPOSE

KNOW PAIN K<u>NO</u>W PURPOSE

LEE ROBBINS

Pain Pushed Me into Purpose

© Copyright 2023 Lee Robbins

specialized training and professional judgment of a health care or mental health care professional.

Neither the author nor the publisher can be held responsible for the use of the information provided within this book. Please always consult a trained professional before making any decision regarding treatment of yourself or others.

For more information, email coach@leerobbins.com

ISBN: 978-1-956884-17-3

Dedication

I want to dedicate this book to . . .

The memory of my mother, Ida Mae Robbins, and all the words of wisdom I now value and use with my children today. I miss you so much!

And to my dad, Lee Robbins, Sr., whom God used to help repurpose my pain by being an example of how significantly a life can be changed through Jesus Christ. Thank you.

Acknowledgements

God – Thank you for saving me from my pain and helping me find my purpose in life. Also, for being a friend that sticks closer than any brother and giving me a heart to serve you people in the mist of my pain.

Kim Robbins – Thank you for sticking with me for over 27 years of marriage making sure you kept the family together by much prayer, through my wrongful conviction, and the kids not having a father for those years. You are an amazing Women of God who is so much smarter than me. The best is yet to come for what God has in store for you in your itinerant ministry. You are having ministry birth pains right now because you are getting ready to deliver your best work ever!

Janae Robbins – Thank you for being intuitive enough to know that I was not working for the government earning 12 cents an hour in prison, but God showed you, as a seven-year-old, my true assignment, as you said, "You work for God, now go work for God," as we dried each other's tears in that visitation room. With those words you really inspired me to do prison reentry ministry when I was so angry at God for taking me away from my family.

Jordan Robbins – Thank you for forgiving me for causing you so much trauma (pain) as a 5-year-old young boy who loved his Daddy but could not really understand why I left you to go to prison when you needed me the most. Greatness is inside of you. Remember, God is going to use your pain to fulfil His purpose for your life. As I have told you many times, one of these days when you wake up your trauma will be over!

Judah Robbins – Thank you for your resilience and how clever you are still today. I remember that day when you at the age of 3, you had such a noble idea about how you could solve my pain in prison and your pain of not having your dad back at home to play Incredible HULK. You said to me after a great visitation, "Dad, you don't have to come home, I can stay here (in prison) with you". Although I was touched by your gesture of sacrifice and love, I had to tell you "NO" which absolutely broke your heart and of course my heart as well.

Lee Robbins Sr. (My dad) – Thank you for being the man of God that you are now today. You taught me hard work and dedication pays off if you just never quit and keep believing in your dreams.

Pastor Brunetta Nelson – Thank you for being such great friend and the publisher of this book. You felt my pain and utilized your publishing skills and of course your awesome team to help me get my story out to the world. I will forever be grateful for you making me believe I really had a book in me that people will want to take the time to read.

Henry Liebring– Thank you for being so kind and patient in listening to my story and pulling out of me the details of my life struggle and business successes and helping me convey them in such a way that any individual and/or business owner can understand my plight in life by relating it to their own.

The Source Church Partners – Thank you for understanding that I am a different kind of pastor who thinks outside of the box of religious tradition and praying for me each week as I deliver the Word God, He has given me for you each Sunday and Wednesday! We will change the world together. Let's Go!

Life Empowerment Enterprise Team – Thank you for helping me empower the "least of these" by providing coaching, jobs, housing, transportation, and better second chances to succeed in life.

Table of Contents

SECTION ONE

THE LABOR PAINS OF PURPOSE

Introduction

I am Pastor Lee Robbins. Before the Lord called me into ministry, I feared rejection, was a people pleaser, and became an overachiever to compensate for my perceived inadequacies. My fear of rejection came from feeling rejected as a child. The low self-esteem that came through my parents' divorce lasted many years.

Trying to compensate for the low self-esteem and help the family's finances, I became a drug dealer. I did things that should have put me behind metal bars or six feet under dirt. While a teenager, I would hold death in my arms. A death that could have been mine. God would use my younger pain to turn my life around. I became a born-again Christian. I went to college and got a bachelor's, then on to seminary for my Masters. I started a business and became an entrepreneur.

I found love, got married, and began having a family. We planted several churches and began pastoring. Life was good. I was a black man who survived the streets, obtained an education, worked hard at owning my own business and pastoring people. Then, I went to prison. I spent three and a half years in the penal system. No, I didn't do it. But it's not what happens to us, it's what we do with what happens to us. I chose to do something with the hand I had been dealt.

All of us have unique childhood experiences that often shape our perspectives and can form the very outcome of our lives, whether good or bad. Childhood can be the most exciting, free, innocent, and joyous times of our lives; but it can also have the ingredient of incredibly painful experiences. Most of us will admit that there are many things we would like the opportunity to go back and change in our early years. But then, who would we be if we did not take the negatives of our lives, the bad things that happen to us, and the situations we've encountered, and allow God to turn them into positives, good things, and God-encounters that can cause us to never wish it had happened any other way?

I can tell you that the circumstances of my life have made me who I am today. All the pains that I have experienced have pushed me into a purpose I didn't see coming and have given me significance in the world and favor with both God and man. And while I wish that I could change some things for others and my loved ones, whose stories I'm about to share, about my own situations . . . I wouldn't change a thing!

Chapter 1: Childhood Shapes Us

I was born in Houston, Texas to Lee and Ida Robbins. My dad, born and raised about 100 miles from Houston, and my mom, a country girl raised by her father, met in Houston and married on March 1, 1958. Both were hard workers. They believed in providing for the household and were dedicated to their work. My dad worked at the same place for 40 years before finally retiring. Mom didn't need to work at first. We lived in a moderately middle-class neighborhood (though it would be considered the "ghettos" some time in later years). Eventually, my mother did need to work to provide and would become a maid until her retirement.

Though my dad worked hard outside the home and my mom worked tirelessly inside the home to provide for and raise their 5 children, their marriage would not last. I was four years old when my dad decided to end the marriage due to irreconcilable differences. No one wants their parents to divorce but it happens. It affects people differently but for me, I felt rejected, though I'm sure I didn't realize it at the time. Sometimes we don't understand how things affect us until later in life. My dad tried to stay in our lives as much as possible but once he had met and married someone new, his time with us became limited. He had a new wife and family and had to focus on providing for them. My brother and I would try to see him at least once a month and on holidays, but it was still very painful to not get that "quality time" every boy needs with their father. Perhaps, because I was named after my father, I thought there should be a closer bond. My mom had a miscarriage before me, so they decided to make me a Junior. I know most parents love their kids equally, but every child likes to feel special, right? I felt special being named after my dad. But then I was sad at the same time because I didn't get to spend more time with him growing up. This was the first pain I remember.

My mom was "cut from a different cloth" altogether. Having been raised by her dad she was a very strong and domineering woman. I'm sure that's one of the reasons my dad decided to part ways. Though we never talked about it, perhaps he was not the quarrelsome type and simply chose to leave rather than get into a physical altercation or just combative arguing. But she was also an alcoholic. She was a very positive person and knew how to make things happen, until she started drinking heavily. Alcoholism is a monster that wreaks havoc on the lives of its victims as well as those connected to them. There's a reason they call liquor "spirits." Eventually my mom would attend AA meetings, become sober, and even become an AA counselor, thanks be to God. But it can have lasting effects on loved ones.

I didn't always like her domineering ways. The nurturing side of her didn't reveal itself too often. Being raised by her dad, she acted like a dad. There was a time I wanted sympathy from my mom so I began hitting my head on the wall, hoping she would stop me and that I would experience her softer side. But no. She told me, "You can knock your brains out if you want to. Just don't tear up my wall." She was tough!

Her boldness often embarrassed us as kids. She would "let us have it" right in front of our friends. She would correct anyone, no matter who it was. She would even tell the neighbors' kids what was on her mind. If she saw someone selling drugs on our corner (we lived in a corner house), she would go outside and tell them to leave saying, "Don't you ever come on my corner selling drugs." She would even grab them by their ear and tell them to leave! I would remind her, "Mamma, don't you know they have 9 mm guns, and they can kill you?" She didn't care and wasn't afraid. I learned how to be tough from my mom. I learned how to persevere, work hard, overcome obstacles, and stand boldly for what I believe. But that domineering side of her hindered my relationships sometimes because if a woman was being strong and tough, I interpreted it as domineering and would emotionally revisit the trauma of my mother's control.

I can't speak for my brothers and sisters but the split of the family, mom's domineering approach to parenting and her alcoholism led to a feeling of rejection for me. Watching her struggle with the divorce, develop an addiction, and must start working outside the home to provide for her 5 children was difficult. I was embarrassed that she would come home from work staggering into the house. The kids in the neighborhood would ridicule us and say, "Your mom's an alcoholic." They would continue mocking me even at school. This brought shame, which caused me to shut down and would lead to low self-esteem.

I was the quieter one in my family, I guess. Everyone assumed that I was shy, but I don't think that I was necessarily shy. I think I just had a fear of talking. Perhaps it was initiated by a fear of rejection from my father leaving, or the simple fear of getting into trouble and my mom getting hold of me. More likely, looking back now, I didn't want to be the reason for more pain. Some thoughtI had "challenges" but I was just being observant and learning to "people please." Fear of rejection, disappointing others, and people pleasing were the negatives from my childhood that I've had to deal with over the years. There are one or two graces, however, that God allowed through this painful period of my life. I became an overachiever. And while that can become a negative, I used it to form a life of adventure and purpose. I learned a good work ethic from my parents and that you can overcome life's obstacles (like my mom did with alcohol) if you are persistent and push past your flesh, allowing Jesus to take the wheel of your life. I may have felt embarrassment many times about my mother's alcoholism but watching her life after that she became my hero.

Childhood shapes us. We can grow and become successful from both the bad and the good of our past. We must become self-aware, learning to use those good qualities, skills, habits, etc. to mold us and shape our future, while allowing the bad experiences, the pain we dealt with, to transform us into a better person. With God's help it can happen. We can be victims of our past or victors for our future. Will you let pain push you into more pain? Or will you allow it to push you into purpose?

Chapter 2: Gone Too Soon

When we think of childhood most of us think of all the things that happened to us until puberty, somewhere around age 12. But, childhood, for me, was gone too soon. It ended at just 8 years old. Like many young, black males without a father at home, I felt like I had to be "the man of the house" and help mom out because she was struggling financially. Not sure if that's how my older brother felt but he had been selling drugs to make his own money. So, he showed me how I could do the same.

My brother and one of my best friends knew how to get to the drug dealers. They gave me a small amount of marijuana to start selling and taught me the trade. As I learned the business, I soon started having my own runners. Remember, I developed an "overachiever" mindset from earlier in life. Though selling drugs was illegal, I was still operating in that mindset. I started making a lot of money selling drugs. I began with small amounts of product then increased the amount as time passed. I was in the streets dealing drugs, trying to bring home money to help my mom. But though she was still drinking at the time, she refused to take any of the money. I would try to convince her that it was going to help but she would say, "Boy, you'd better stop selling those drugs. That's what you'd better stop doing."

Here I was, the one who was trying to not cause my mom any problems, the overachiever, cooking marijuana in my mom's oven. She was trying to recover from alcohol, keep her family together, and move into the healing process, and I was selling drugs. Surprisingly, I never got into trouble with the law. I sold drugs "under the radar" for years. Of course, I later would come to realize that this is really a slow set up to catch dealers. Law enforcement would let you sell for 2-3 years while building a case against you and your enterprise. Thank God it was just marijuana and not crack! No matter what drug it was, I know that it was God alone who kept me from an earlier "adventure" into the prison system. I broke the law; I just didn't get caught.

Sadly, something was about to take place that would begin to change me, more than the possibility of getting caught could have ever done. During this time of dealing drugs people would often have what we called "house parties." Some of us weren't old enough to go to clubs so we went to house parties around the area. One night, my "posse" at the time, and myself, were headed to one of these parties. Now, sometime before this my brother, my best friend, and I were at the basketball courts. While in play my brother used a "tackle technique" to block someone on the other team from making the basket. Then it got ugly. A fight ensued, my friend and I jumped in, someone's tooth got knocked out, and my brother cut one of the guys. My younger brother protected me, and the other guy had to go get stitches. Now we had enemies.

Back to the party. As we entered this party, two guys in front of me and two behind me saw the guy from the court fight. He was at the party too. He noticed us and pulled out a gun, pointed it my way, and fired. There was no time to think or take cover. The bullet hits my best friend who was walking in front of me and he falls back into my arms. I believe he took a bullet with my name on it. He was losing a lot of blood as I held onto him. I held him as I watched life leave his body and he took his last breath. He died, right there in my arms.

I was only 14 years old. By this time, I have experienced a lot of personal pain; but holding someone in your arms as they pass, especially your closest friend, would have to be one of the highest pain points in life and something no one, especially a young person, should ever have to experience. This profound incident would begin my process of change for good. Change comes slowly sometimes. I still sold drugs, even after the "house party" incident. My mom tried to get me to stop. But this surreal experience taught me more lessons than I wanted to learn. Raising kids is tough. My wife used to sing a song to our kids when they kept saying "mamma, mamma." She would sing some country song that said "Mamma don't let your babies grow up to be cowboys. Don't let 'em pick guitars and drive them old trucks. Make 'em be doctors and lawyers and such."

It was just a funny response because they kept saying her name. But truly, we, as parents, must raise our kids to make the most of their lives. Let's not wait until they experience devastating pain. But even if they do, we know that God can move in their life and use those experiences for good. I'm always amazed at how God does that. One may have died in my arms, but later another would live again.

Chapter 3: Knowledge is Power

At 14, I was working at a car wash. I didn't really need the money because I was making plenty by selling drugs. But I needed a cover to camouflage my "drug money." Whether or not people knew I sold drugs they knew Friday was payday. Fridays were when the "cash bandits" showed up on the scene.

One Friday I was walking home from work, having just cashed my check. I noticed a guy following me. He would cross the street when I did and move each direction I would move. I knew he was one of those "cash bandits." Before I could even think he moved up behind me and put a 9 mm Glock to my head. I said, "I know what you want." I grabbed my wallet and handed it to him. He simply said, "Okay," and took the cash. I told him, "I don't want to apply for another social security card." I was trying to get that back at least. I carried that card in my wallet in those days because it was the only way to cash my check. He said, "Shut up, or I'll blow your brains out." I said, "I just want to keep the card for my next check." He told me, "If you turn around, I'm going to blow your head off." I turned away from him. Then, because of curiosity I guess, or maybe I didn't believe he would shoot me, I quickly turned back around and saw that he was gone. We were in an alley with only one way out and he was nowhere to be seen. To me, this was a supernatural intervention. God was trying to get my attention. He was up to something and protected me in what could have been the end of me.

During this period of my life, I noticed things I hadn't really paid attention to previously. My oldest sister met a young man who knew the Lord. She was now living the "straight and narrow" as they say. I admired her for that and watching her live for Jesus created a curiosity in me. Also, I had started dating a girl about four years my senior, in my freshman year. She had a toddler but that didn't bother me. I loved her and the baby and was willing to stay the course. She soon started to go to church with my sister. I wasn't really interested in all that "church stuff." But one day I found my girlfriend's diary. Now, I know that should have been private, but I was nosey and wanted to see what she wrote in her diary. Maybe there was something in there about me, or us. Then I saw where she had written, "I LOVE JESUS. I CAN'T WAIT TO BE WITH YOU". You may not believe this but I really didn't know anything about Jesus at the time, so I read this with a Spanish pronunciation. So, to me, it said, "I LOVE (HAY-SOOS)." I wanted to know who "Hay-Soos" was because I wanted to go beat him up for trying to take my girl. Ignorance is not bliss.

With this newfound love my girlfriend had, things began to change between us. Having been exposed to sexual impositions at the early age of 8, my relationships involved promiscuity. But my girlfriend didn't want to have sex anymore outside of marriage. She didn't even want to kiss anymore! She had gone "all in." As I watched those around me change their lifestyles, I began to realize something had to shift for me too. The death of my best friend was a turning point. Being face to face with death on several occasions in my life and not knowing God said to me "you need to change." I told myself, "If I can't make the changes on my own, I will give God a try." And I did.

I didn't seem to have the willpower to overcome the drug situation. I wasn't just selling dope; I was also smoking it. I remember saying to God, "If I can stop smoking weed on my own within 30 days, I don't really need you. But if I can't, I will give you a try." I did really well. I was confident that I could stop smoking on my own. I had stopped smoking all the way up to the 29th day. Then, on day 30, I gave in and renewed my drug dealing and dope smoking habits. I knew then that willpower was not enough to get me through it. I realized that I had a problem and perhaps I needed to seek a higher power to help me.

I went to church the next Sunday with a deliberate commitment that I would meet God. It didn't matter to me at all what was being preached. It just didn't matter. All I knew was that I was going to get saved that day. After the preaching ended, I ran down to the altar. I was crying and saying, "I want to be saved, I want to be saved. I must be saved. I got to be saved." Then that precious pastor shared with me, for the first time in my life, a clear presentation of the gospel, what it means to be saved, and he "led me to the Lord."

The following day, the scales fell from my eyes. I was born again. A new life in Christ was birthed in me. I could finally understand why my loved ones wanted to live differently. I, too, went "all in." At this point I was 15 years old, attending church every time the doors were open. I understood that my heavenly Father loved me "just as I am." I don't have to "people please," or feel rejected. When I understood this, I immediately wanted to reach out to my dad. I wanted to reconcile with him and restore our relationship. I had unforgiveness and bitterness in my heart because of the pain I had experienced when he left. I needed to forgive my dad. And I did.

I gave up drugs, gave up my old lifestyle, and gave up my Glocks. I gave it all up. I said, "This is my life now." One of the most encouraging things about being on the streets is that no one wants to be there, so when someone gets out, they are happy for that person. They were happy for me. They were glad and supportive that I had changed my life. When someone would offer drugs to me, others would stand up and say, "No, don't offer that to him." Though they may have still been doing or selling drugs they spoke on my behalf.

While still in high school, I became a youth pastor for a local church, taught Sunday school and was ordained at the age of 17. My grades in school improved and I was on the honor roll. I was still trying to be an overachiever. I was active in sports. I played basketball, baseball, and ran on the track team. I was even the star running back on the football team. I even joined the school drama team. I still functioned off the desire to not disappoint people. My inner pain and insecurity didn't allow me to be true to myself. I HAD to please others. I wanted to be the best; not because I was competitive but because I thought being the best was my path to please others.

Pleasing others makes you feel liked, or even loved. Most of us battle this at some point in our lives. But God accepts us for who we are, not what we do. Faith is what pleases God. If you are like I was and always trying to please others, I pray that you come to understand that God created you just like you are and you don't have to become a "be all" to everyone to win His approval. This has been an ongoing learning curve for me. Only recently have I come to fully understand how I allowed the pain of my childhood to shape my feelings of rejection, insecurity, and people pleasing.

As I look back over the years, I can clearly see God at work in my life. Sometimes pain doesn't seem like it has any purpose; especially when you are in the middle of the fire. But there's a beautiful scripture (captured in a song by Bobby McFarland) that says," No discipline seems pleasant at the time, but painful; later on, however, it produces a harvest of righteousness and peace for those who have been trained by it" (Hebrews 12:11). That reminds me of those times my mom used to whip us. Or maybe I should say "whoop." She'd send me out to get a switch and I'd start picking the leaves off on the walk back saying, "she loves me, she loves me not." It seemed to end on "not." Then she would say, "I'm doing this because I love you." I would respond, "Then don't love me so much, Mamma!" She even whipped me when I didn't reach my grade potential. I made a "C" once, thinking it was better than my brother's "D." But she said she whipped me because my potential was an "A." You know, God is like that sometimes it seems. We wonder why others don't have to endure the pain that we do. But God sees our potential and disciplines us accordingly. There IS purpose in your pain. Even in that "whoopin'."

God was up to something. Knowledge is power, they say. What you don't know can kill you, or at the very least, stop you from living up to your potential in life. God had more in store for me and he moved through people and situations in my life to get me to the place he wanted for me all along. He provides a "way of escape" the Bible says. It is up to us to take the route provided. He opened an opportunity for me that I wasn't expecting.

Before high school graduation I had a life-altering conversation with one of my teachers. He was an Asian man teaching at Jesse H. Jones High School, but I can't recall his name. What he did for me would change the trajectory of my life. One day, he asked me about my future and what I was going to do after high school. I said, "I'm just going to get a job." I hadn't considered secondary education. I thought people like me, who had no money, couldn't attend college. My teacher responded with, "No, you can go to college." I couldn't believe it. He explained to me how I could go to school on a Pell Grant, got me the paperwork, and I applied. I got accepted to the University of Houston, where my entire tuition was paid for by the Pell Grant. I graduated with a Bachelor's degree in Business Computer Information Systems with a dual degree in accounting. Though I can't recall that teacher's name, I am forever grateful for what he did for me. Learn what you can from life experiences, from mentors, and especially from the Word of God. Learn, so you can reach your potential.

Chapter 4: A Blueprint for Manhood

Over the years my mom and I developed a great relationship. Before she gave her life to Christ she was sold on AA. I would attend meetings with her and everyone would stand up and say their name then claim they were still alcoholics. I understood what they were trying to do but when you know God that kind of mindset is contrary to Him, His Word, and how He sees us it's difficult to keep your mouth shut. My past is my past. I am a new creation. Therefore, I don't take on the titles of my past. When it came to my turn to say my name I would say, "Hi, my name is Lee and I'm born again and delivered by the blood of Jesus!" I'm sure my mother wanted to roll her eyes at me. But I was a new man, and I couldn't stay quiet about what the Lord had done for me. And being a new man, I began to search for male role models.

I mean, my mom was tough, but she wasn't a man. And I still hadn't really built a strong relationship with my dad yet. I would observe other men in the Church, develop mentors, and often think about what it meant to be a "man" or "man of God." I have often thought about the question "What makes a man?" God said, "Let us remain in our own image and likeness." I know that this is referring to "mankind", but I like to sometimes make it personal. When I work with boys and men or when I'm working in prisons with incarcerated men, I often refer to this scripture to help men see themselves as God sees them and not as the world sees them. Oftentimes, men define their manhood by how many women they have slept with, or by their physical capabilities. Or they may define themselves by the amount of money they make, regardless of how they make it. Still, they may feel that aggression makes them a man, how many children they produce, or how good they are at something. None of this denotes that we are men or supports how God created us. We are made in the image of God. How God sees us is how we should see ourselves. What He does as a Father, as a Husband ɓ the Church, is the ultimate "role model" for what it means to be a man and how we should portray our manhood.

God has the blueprint for manhood. Once we understand our relationship with the Lord, He'll show us how to be in relationships with others. This helped me tremendously in reconciling with my dad. While I was in college, I needed a place to stay because my mom always told us that once you leave the house don't plan on coming back to live there again. So, my dad allowed me to come and stay with him. That's when I really got the chance to make amends with him. I shared with him how I felt about him leaving us and the trauma that created in our lives, or at least mine. I told him about my pain and how much it had hurt when he left. We cried together and I began to tell him about my new relationship with Jesus Christ. I told him that he could receive Christ too. I later shared the gospel with him, and he accepted the Lord.

Our relationship was much better, and we were closer now. I was beginning to heal. Once my father became a Believer, he would eventually go on to lead his family to the Lord, minister to his siblings who either recommitted their lives to the Lord or may have received Him for the first time. He joined his father-in-law's church and remained there for the next 40 years or so. It was beautiful to watch God use my dad in that way.

I later had the privilege of also leading my mother to the Lord. When you find purpose in life your pain is no longer seen as pain but as a process. Just as a woman may experience pain in labor, the pain is dismissed once she experiences the joy of that beautiful baby. That's what I'm told anyway. And that's what the Word of God says.

Chapter 5: The Call

So, life for me started kind of rocky. I learned what to do and what not to do in many situations. God intervened on my behalf many times. I've shared several of them thus far. One that should have gotten me closer to God early on was when I attended camp in the 5th grade. As for my people pleasing, scared of rejection feelings, I had developed I didn't want the other kids to know that I couldn't swim. So, I thought, I'll just jump close to the edge and when I come up, I'll grab the side of the pool and I will be good. But we know things don't always turn out like we think they will and sometimes our "wisdom" falls far short. They dared me to jump. I couldn't swim. But I had a plan. My plan failed. I ended up in the middle of the pool, gasping for air and trying to stay afloat. I went down once, twice, then a third time.

My life flashed before me. I was going to die. I was also thinking I would end up in hell because I didn't know

God. But I threw my arm out of the water one last time and someone grabbed me by the hand and gently moved me to the side of the pool. But when I looked up there was no one there. God must have sent an angel to carry me over to the edge.

There are many more stories I could talk about the goodness of God and His saving grace. But let's move forward. All my childhood experiences that caused me pain were transforming into God's purpose for my life. God was mending the broken pieces and creating the masterpiece, the picture for my life. Did you know that God says you are His masterpiece, created in Christ to do good works? He gives beauty for ashes and the oil of gladness for the spirit of heaviness.

From the day of my salvation at age 15 to about age 20 life moved fast. I finished high school, went on to college, graduated college, worked as a youth pastor, taught Sunday school, became a personal minister to a local pastor and began to think about my future. I felt the call to preach. I was passionate about the Word, about helping people to know Jesus, to know this freedom that I experienced. I was working in the accounting department for a large corporation, making quite a bit of money. But the Holy Spirit was moving in my heart to do more for God's Kingdom. At 22, I preached my first message. But I knew there was more.

I felt a desire to go to seminary. I hadn't told my pastor yet but Oral Roberts' son, Richard, came to visit our church and gave a small scholarship for the pastor's choosing to attend Oral Roberts University. While I was in the prayer line, the pastor had a "word of knowledge" and said, "I'm just sure you want to go to school, and this scholarship belongs to you." Not having said anything to him I knew this was God's confirmation to me to attend seminary. I soon left my job and moved to Tulsa, Oklahoma.

Chapter 6: The Last Hoorah

There were a lot of transitions with my move to Tulsa. Some financial, some personal, and some spiritual. I was attending what is referred to as a "spirit-filled" institution and I wasn't even sure I believed in the "baptism of the Holy Spirit." I had seen the difference in those around me and I had been a personal minister for two years in a spirit-filled church. But I was chosen to go this route and I knew God had something more in store for me. I was excited about attending ORU. It's the "Yale" of Christian schools. It has an excellent scholastic reputation and is quite diverse. People from many countries attend there.

I had saved some money for the move to Tulsa but needed income to live there and have the time necessary to get the schoolwork done. Plus, I intended on finding a church where I could serve, and chapel services were twice a week on campus. It was a busy life. I decided to use my education in accounting and computers and start a bookkeeping business. I did bookkeeping, accounting, and taxes. I quickly developed a following with a niche market: barbers and beauticians. I worked diligently for my clientele and developed an excellent reputation in both my business and church life. In a relatively short time, I had over a thousand clients. I was doing well.

Many things happened during my time at ORU. I met Kim, my wife, while there. We were taking a summer class in Greek. This was not my area, and I was glad the teacher suggested we find 2 other study partners and meet once or twice a week. Kim, I, and a fellow church goer of mine, Ed, started meeting together. Ed disappeared from our meetings at some point during the summer and then it was just me and Kim. She hates it when I try to joke about our times starting out 100% study and then later spending more time on us. Of course, she was doing most of the tutoring since Greek was definitely "Greek" to me. She was just trying to get through the course and help me pass.

Sidenote here: Seminary was difficult, and I was nt getting very good grades when I first started. Then, I finally had an encounter in the prayer tower. The baptism of the Holy Spirit became real to me. I was forever changed. And incredibly my grades went from C's to A's after that. You never know what can happen when God gets hold of you!

Kim and I dated, then married in the summer of 1996. I graduated in 1997 and she in 1998. The business was doing well. I had an office in Tulsa and was able to hire an employee. Kim and I moved to Georgia after graduating and I left the office in the care of this new hire. I tried to get someone skilled in accounting to take the office, but I could not meet their salary requirements when moving to a new state and opening offices there. He was a youth leader under my oversight as youth pastor in our church and he had two small kids while his wife was pregnant with their third. He had just lost his job and we felt for their family and those precious children. I took him on because he was determined to learn and asked for nothing in return. After seeing his dedication, I began to pay him so he could care for his family. We trusted him because he was a believer, and we knew him. Or at least we thought we did. In hindsight, he had told us his job fired him for driving the company truck outside of the designated boundaries. Obviously, he had an integrity issue; but somehow, we didn't catch that.

We moved to the Atlanta, Georgia area and I extended my business. Robbins & Associates was now in two states with multiple offices, and I decided to franchise the business. Though pastoring was the plan, I enjoyed seeing the business flourish. I no longer felt insecure because my business was thriving. I was confident now. I had built a business with multiple offices and several employees.

During this transition to a new state, new family, and more office extensions, we also planted a church. Crossroads International Church was our heart and passion. Some of our best years were spent with these wonderful, supportive, Jesus-loving people. There are many more stories I could share about pastoring, church planting, and such but I want to move to the greatest pain in my life that propelled me into God's purpose for me. I will say here though, that if your pain came through "church hurt" or through people you trusted, God can heal it and take you into a greater place if you let Him.

So, the church was moving along, and my business was still flourishing. However, I had some concerns about leaving my Tulsa office in the hands of this young man. My wife had even mentioned it on the move to Georgia. She suggested just closing it down. We had started a daycare and left it in the hands of his wife, so she felt they would be fine until he found other employment. But I didn't do that. The Lord had even directed me about a year later to just close the Tulsa office. But I didn't. I cannot stress enough the importance of obeying God when you know He's telling you something. It can save you from a lot of hurt and possibly from death itself.

Life is good . . . until it isn't! We still had our church, our offices, and employees. Most importantly, it's 2003 and Kim and I just had our third child. But sometimes with joy there comes sorrow. My mother passed about 2 months to the day after Judah was born. I officiated her funeral. It was a very tough request to fulfill. But earlier that year, just before the birth of our child, I was sent a piece of mail I was told would be coming. Receiving mail in the prison system is a blessing. This was not that! In this thick, yellow envelope was a legal document stating that I was being indicted for filing fraudulent returns. My Tulsa employee was listed on the document as co-defendant. This meant that conspiracy charges were also being filed against us. I was brought in through this conspiracy charge and tied to 15 of 65 counts of fraud.

I felt sick reading that document. I knew something was coming but I had no idea, nor would have ever thought something like this would happen. I never got in trouble when selling illegal drugs. But here I am, a pastor, entrepreneur, and business owner, trying to take care of my family, my church, and another believer in Christ and his family, and I'm being indicted for a crime I did not commit. I couldn't see how anything good could come from this if I were found guilty. But God always has a plan.

Chapter 7: The Agony of Defeat

I've never had a defeatist mindset. Always the optimist, positive, everything is possible kind of person would probably describe me much better. I was never one to really admit to defeat. Call it pride, stubbornest, or a lot of my mamma in me but I definitely wasn't going down without a fight!

So much happened so fast during the year I was preparing for trial. The agents were interrogating my friends, combing over documents, trying to build their case. Some of the things that happened with this case are shocking and some were downright scary. But I trusted God to see me through it. It also helped to have family support.

People often talk about their in-laws in a negative light. But I have the best in-laws. My wife's parents believed in my innocence and supported me every step of the way. They even went so far as to sell a lake house condo they had purchased to be closer to their kids and their kids' families just to help pay my legal fees. I hated that they had to do that. I may never be able to repay them in this lifetime, but I am grateful for their support and all they did for me and our family. I know they were mostly looking after their daughter and grandkids probably, but I also know they believed in me and I don't take for granted how they tried to get me the best lawyer they could afford to keep me from the fate of prison.

Yes, that was my fate. Prison. I go into more detail about my trial and that whole process later in the book; but I never would have thought I would ever find myself on the other side of the prison walls. Kim and I lived down the road from Philips State Prison and I would often mention how I would like to do prison ministry and that I should try to see if I could get permission to go into Philips since it was nearby. Be careful what you wish for, right? Perhaps I should have been clearer with God.

"Lord, I meant go minister in prison and leave the SAME DAY!"

I had to tell my church the news. I had not really said anything because I was believing for the truth to be told and not be found guilty. However, once they sentenced me, I had to tell our congregation that I would be leaving in a month. They were shocked. Some were upset that we hadn't told them. But how do you tell people you serve in a pastoral setting that you're being indicted on fraud and may have to serve time in a federal prison camp? There is no easy way to do that.

But our church stood by us and believed with us that our appeal would be granted, and I would return in 3 months. That did not happen. I believe I preached one of the best messages I've ever preached on my last Sunday in the pulpit. The title of my message was, "I Am a Posterity to Your Prosperity." It was a Joseph's story. That's how I felt. The meaning of posterity for me was "a present suffering for the deliverance of a future generation."

Joseph was his family's posterity. He went through what he went through for the benefit of others. It was a powerful message if I do say so myself. It was a very solemn moment. But the people stood with us and supported us. It was a tearful and heartfelt time for sure.

Kim continued to pastor while I was gone. But when I did not win the appeal people started to see it as a sign from God that it was time to go. She was homeschooling two of our kids while trying to chase a busy 2-year-old around the house. She also handled the "business" of the church as well as preached every Sunday and Wednesday. My wife had to make a lot of decisions quickly and did so with grace. She enjoyed pastoring and caring for the people, preaching God's Word, and ensuring our kids were well cared for; however, only the faithful few remained with her. After about 7 months, Kim made the decision to shut the doors of the church and focus on the kids and her itinerant ministry.

Financially, Kim did well. She sold everything she could to make sure our bills were paid. Once she was out of resources and options, her parents helped with the rest. I wish that I could say the family of God came to our rescue and helped my wife in this time of need. While several of our church members did sow into her financially for a few months, and my family tried to gather some money together to help as well, there really was no "lifeline" to assist her with the necessary resources to care for three kids, a nice home, and a vehicle. She really couldn't go to work because there was no one to watch the kids so she could do an interview. And even if she had gotten a job, the daycare costs for three kids would have nearly equaled her pay and she wouldn't be left with much after that. Sometimes people forget that when anyone is incarcerated, their families usually are too, in some way. God still provided. Checks would appear in the mail from unexpected sources, just in time to pay a bill. Businesses that owed us, insurance adjustments or claims that hit just in time, and believers who God spoke to specifically to help in this difficult season.

Our children did not quite know what was going on with me when I left. They were used to me traveling so we dropped them off at a church member's home and told them I would be gone for a while. Again, we thought I would be out on appeal in 3 months. I hugged them tightly and reassured them I would be back as soon as I could. Then, Kim and I continued the 45-minute drive to Atlanta's Federal Prison Camp. The camp looked like something out of the history books. It was drizzling rain, so the sky was cloudy. This brought the mood down even further.

We pulled into the gate where I was directed to offload and mandated to report on time. We sat there for a moment. Then, a trail of men began lining up at the same door I was to enter. They were looking our way, making things incredibly awkward. Kim was ready to leave at that point. I gave her a hug and a kiss and told her to "Go ahead, I'll be fine." She was headed home, and I was headed

behind the wire.

SECTION 2

PRISON – WHEN PURPOSE SUPERSEDES PAIN

Chapter 8: Prison

Processing

Processing (the term is a bit ironic) to become Atlanta Federal Prison Camp Inmate #09534-062 took the better part of the day. I had to remove my street clothes and turn them in to be stored. I carried a small Bible with me which I was also required to surrender, as all books must come only through the mail (ultimately, I was able to keep the bible, which was the first of many small mercies I received).

In place of my civilian clothes, I was issued two sets of "greens," a khaki top and pants that would become my uniform for the next two-and-a-half years (actually, they were literally green, not khaki. To this day, I won't buy anything that color of green). I was then handed a very thin sheet which was the extent of my bedding. On cold nights, we learned to wear every article of clothing we had to stay warm. I was assigned my bunk inside a dormitory of approximately seventy other cast-off souls, all weighing and appraising my presence without a word. Too awkward to stare back, I could only self-consciously speculate what their vacant expressions conveyed.

My First Night

The lights shut off at exactly 11 p.m. That first night, I stretched out on my bunk and cried in my soul as tears streamed quietly down my face. The drop off this morning already felt like a lifetime ago.

In the concealment of darkness, my soul cried to the Lord, *"Why have you forsaken me? I am innocent!"* My grief was deafening in my spirit, but silent to those around me. I knew instinctively, "You can't show weakness here."

When the lights went out, the chorus of flatulence began. I learned there's a superhuman ability of prisoners to refrain from farting until darkness because that allows for anonymity. As soon as the lights were shut off, the toots and horns were immediate, creating a cacophony like the sounds of a freeway. I easily visualized the type of vehicle from which each sound might originate.

I could hear blaring base-model sedans, rumbling sports cars, bellowing diesel truck horns, and the occasional squeak of a Fiat. The image was inescapably hilarious, and I couldn't help musing who in the room was "driving" the hamster mobile.

Morning Wake-Up

Wake-up came early and suddenly as the lights flashed on and someone shouted, *"twelve,"* which I later learn is code for, "Police are coming." Then someone else yelled, "Count time!" which is something done three times every day to ensure everyone is accounted for and no one has escaped.

This being my first count, I had no idea that you must stand at attention the whole time until count has cleared (meaning, everyone has been tallied and no one is missing). This could take 45 minutes or more. On this first day, I waited and sat on my bunk to be added to the count.

I was soon viciously corrected by an officer who I later learned was named Mr. White. He was the one nobody dared "mess with" or underestimate. He had a reputation for hating prisoners and he would send them to the hole every chance he could find. He was an older man who had been working as a Correctional Officer (C.O.) with the prison for a very long time and seemed miserable; I believe his sole purpose was to make others as miserable as him.

When I didn't stand for count, as no one had told me the rules yet, he banged on my cubicle and began cursing at me. *"You M.F.'er, if you don't stand, I will show you how in the hole!* I was already dazed and fatigued from almost no sleep, and he was "breaking me in" and making sure I understood his dominance as the "tough guy." My punishment for failing to stand was picking up the cigarette butts left by the prison officers which were scattered around the compound.

Breakfast

Breakfast was the next torment to be endured. We stood outside the chow hall in a long line, shivering in the biting air until it was our turn to hastily slam down the "foodstuff" before we were ordered back outside. Five minutes was deemed plenty of time to eat, chew and swallow what was on your plate.

The morning's meal was obviously leftovers, likely the unheated remains from some other institution's subpar offering passed along to fill our stomachs. The day's menu included eggs (probably powdered), a biscuit too hard b possibly eat in five minutes, and a carton of milk.

The number of rats eating alongside us was so numerous, there was no effort for concealment, which made me wonder if that was pepper or rat droppings in my scrambled egg product.

The smell inside the chow hall was so putrid, I seriously couldn't tell if the milk in my tiny carton was sour or if it was just the stench of the place. As I threw up in the hall after I left the building, I knew that the milk was indeed expired … and likely for some time.

My First Three Months

I suffered the misery of a damned soul for the first three months. I can remember looking at the barbed wire fence and feeling the "barbed wire sickness." It's a real thing that everyone experiences. The wire whispers, *"You're not going anywhere!"* It doesn't matter if you are in for 10 years, 30 years, or life, you are simply *not going anywhere*!! With that realization, a weakness spreads over your body, your immune system shuts down, and you feel like dying. You know you're not free, and when you accept that, your mind becomes incarcerated, and your emotions are imprisoned as well.

I was dying in my spirit. I couldn't accept my fate. My anger towards God went unchecked. I didn't belong in this savage place. I had been a pastor whose only desire was to serve people. My only dream, my sole purpose in life, was to love and serve people, and that's just what Kim and I were doing up until I got locked up in this prison purgatory.

Worries

I worried about our congregation. What would happen to it? Would the congregation survive? How would my family survive, as Kim had not worked outside the home since we left Tulsa.

All the roles I filled as a pastor, husband, and father had been my vision, my passion, my destiny. And now, who was I? Just a prisoner who made 12 cents an hour manufacturing mattresses. I felt hopeless; and like in Dante's *Inferno*," hopelessness is the gateway to hell."

Family Visitation

Visitation with my family was the best and hardest moment of my prison experience.

Being able to spend time with our family members was the greatest excitement of our lives. We would carefully prepare, clean up, and look nice, just waiting to hear our names called through the speaker system. "Robbins, you have a visitor!"

I could have been told I had won the lottery, and the enthusiasm wouldn't be any greater each time that was announced. There's something about hearing your name that says you are important in a place hell-bent on telling you otherwise every moment of your confinement. It's a prestigious thing to have a family that visits you, especially because so many have no one to visit them.

Some people had burned all their bridges and had no mail or visitation through their entire incarceration. But these men were still rooting for me. If your name is called and you happen to be in the restroom, someone will come running to get you shouting, "Go, go, go! You know you want that visit!"

You wait to see your loved ones. There's a space carved out to meet with them in the prison. You can't sit on the same side but must face each other across the table. The prison doesn't want you even touching, no scenes of kissing outside of an initial hug and peck.

My kids loved coming to visitation, especially because it was their treat time. We had a vending machine with goodies and my children looked forward to the visits because kids love snacks, of course; so, my wife would make sure they got that with me on those visitation days. She would slip me quarters to buy the treats, so I could feel and appear like I was doing something for them. Buying candy from the vending machine for my kids is what I looked forward to all week.

My family usually visited me once a week for most of my incarceration. We would talk through all the school stuff, the victories, and any mishaps. Kim had those three kids keeping her very busy.

We had been telling the children that I was working for the government, on a mission, and couldn't come home yet, (which was partially true). We weren't sure they would understand prison and how I got there because they were so young. But on one particular visit, my oldest daughter became curious and asked me, "Daddy, is this a prison? Why are you here?" Kim entertained the boys while I took her aside and away from the crowd and began to describe how I got there. It was an emotional moment.

As I was explaining it to her, she asked, "So Daddy, you mean you aren't supposed to be here? You are innocent? That isn't right! These people are holding you!" I could see anger rise in her. She went through a series of emotions all at once before me. She was mad that I was being kept there, and she was mad at the guy that did it. Then she concluded, "You got to do God's work. God has you here."

Once she understood that God had a reason for me to be there, at eight years old she became my coach and was encouraging me. Children are closer to God than we are at times. They are right out of Heaven, so innocent and pure.

I then took my oldest son aside and shared with him what I thought he would understand. He has always been a very "matter of fact" kind of kid. He accepted what was going on and why I was there and that I was working for the Lord, even in the midst of all of this. But I knew that, like when I was young, he was internalizing his pain. I am sure he was hurting on the inside more than perhaps even I did at his age. He and I were very close prior to going to prison. And while I believe all my children experienced a high level of trauma due to my incarceration, he more significantly perhaps because he didn't know what to do with his pain.

A Sad Visit with My Three-Year-Old Son

The saddest moment of my entire incarceration happened one day at the end of visitation.

My three-year-old son came up with a solution. He was so sincere and happy, knowing he had an answer. Dressed in green, becoming quite buff and in the best shape of my life from working out, I played "Incredible Hulk" with my kids when they came to visit. I would hit my hand or leg and make the transformation into the green angry monster that is the Incredible Hulk right in front of them, scooping them up, throwing them in the air, and chasing my screaming, giggling children around visitation. At the end of our visit one day, my young son jubilantly exclaimed, "Since you can't come home; I will stay here, and we can play Incredible Hulk all the time!"

"No son, we can't," I gently corrected. He burst ot crying. It wasn't weeping, it was a wail that echoed throughout the entire visitation room and my wife had to drag him out, pulling him from holding the security check, while screaming, "I want my daddy! I want my daddy! No one could calm him down. The female warden and officers were crying, other inmates were crying, because this curly-headed mixed kid was being dragged out howling for his daddy. He wasn't having it. We all watched him through the gates and the barbed wire fence as he was loaded up and driven away. We were all crying and trying to console each other. I was overcome with the pain of my emotional child wanting his daddy. My separation from my dad when I was little was traumatic in its own way.

But watching my children go through this pain was heart wrenching. In my opinion, the whole family was surviving prison pain though they were free physically. It was a financial strain as well as an emotional one.

Prison Was Often Emotionally Difficult

It wasn't just the sadness of watching my children endure my absence, there were other things that brought sorrow behind the wire. While I would eventually find purpose and even times of joy as I watched the transformation of the people around me, prison life still had its moments of tragedy and excruciating sadness.

An inmate died in prison with Cancer

A fellow inmate had played in the GAP Band and served 18 years in prison. He was diagnosed with cancer with only six months left to live, and just six months left on his sentence. We worked hard to get him to be able to spend the last six months with his family. We petitioned the warden, congressmen, everyone, as I watched him get thinner and thinner, weaker, and weaker. I would sit at his bedside and pray with him. I promised to do my best and use the connections I had on the outside. In the end he was told, "No, you are going to die in prison."

When I passed their answer on to him, he was already feeling hopeless, and I watched him die that day before his body joined him. He died emotionally. He had been our musician in our prison church and was so faithful. I was terribly pained to give him that news and say that we had failed.

Can't leave to go to your son's funeral

We had a "track" where we could walk, run, or exercise. This was not like most tracks you might envision, but it was our momentary way to feel like life was in motion. We would spend time walking around the tracking, talking about our lives and what was going on with us. We probably walked 10 miles sometimes and didn't even realize it. One of the guys had a son who had been killed. He was murdered in Atlanta and left in a ditch.

He was talking and telling his story. He said he didn't know if he could make it through this pain. He was suicidal. I'm not a counselor and I don't know how they might have talked with him; but I know Jesus. We're talking and he's telling me his story. We are crying together as we continue moving around the track. I felt his pain because I have two sons of my own and I couldn't imagine something like this happening to one of them. He had lost his only son. It was a cruel death too. To add to his pain, I'm sure you can guess ... he could not go to the funeral. The prison authorities would not let him attend because they considered him a "risk." Everyone knew about that decision, and it was very sad.

Some people get buried in the back of the prison

Some people don't have family to come and get their bodies when they die. When that happens in the facility, when the person doesn't have a proper funeral, they bury the body in the back. Literally, they don't get to have a funeral. Sometimes we would have a memorial service without the body being there to help people get closure.

12 Cents an Hour

You can't get much for the work you do in prison. Many people may think you shouldn't get paid anything. But some of those who are incarcerated wouldn't be able to talk to the outside world or get a decent snack in between the mess hall meals if they didn't have a few dollars on their books. My family couldn't really afford to send money to my account because my wife was busy making sure the bills were getting paid at home. Plus, growing up like I did I knew how to make it on very little. This was definitely "very little!" I was working for 12 cents an hour in the federal prison.

I worked 40 hours a week, which resulted in $25 a month. I used $15 to call and talk with my wife and kids. Each time you call you get 15 very precious minutes. I could only afford to call about once a week; but that was better than none for sure. I avoided using that limited time on the phone to discipline the kids. My wife may have needed that at times and if so, I would give them gentle reminders. But there were better discussions to have during those 15 minutes. I loved those few moments I had to speak with my family. I wished I could have afforded more of them. I used the remaining $10 for the commissary to get a candy bar or snack on occasion.

Getting Mail in Prison

My dad would write to me from time to time. I didn't hear much from anyone else. Of course, too many on the outside two or three years in prison is nothing. I may not have even spoken to loved ones that often so it doesn't really seem like it would be a big deal.

But when you are in a place where you can go nowhere and are experiencing the "horrors" of the penal system, it helps to hear from others and to know that someone is thinking about you. Getting mail in prison is a very prestigious thing. There are guys who never get mail, but they go to mail call. They may not have anyone on the outside who cares or perhaps people who cared are now deceased. But they come to mail call because they have some hope that somebody will send them something.

Some guys got 10 pieces of mail and some guys got zero. If a man received a lot of mail, everyone would think he's important because he has 10 people caring about him. We all wanted to feel like that. I understood this and decided to coordinate with my wife to find "pen pals" for some of the residents who did not get any mail. This was set up as a surprise for them. When these letters arrived, I watched these guys show up for mail call, expecting nothing really, but then hearing their name called that only rejoice with them. We were happy for them.

They didn't know who sent it, but it didn't matter. They were grateful someone cared. My wife wrote a few of those letters herself. These men would read them over and over and absorb the heartfelt affirmations and encouragement that was written on the pages. They were so thankful for the love. God was glorified through this. These letters were like a prized possession to them and, as such, they stored them safely with their belongings.

Chapter 9: THE SHIFT

Why Do Bad Things Happen to Good People?

While going about the day-to-day routines at my new accommodation, I would hear the age-old question continually run through my mind, "Why do bad things happen to good people?" I was not just innocent; I was doing good things! I think most of us have thought once or twice in our lives, "Why me, Lord?"

With mercy and patience God answered me. He said, "Who said you are good? There's no one good, not one." I was reminded that, though I was innocent, I wasn't sinless. This is when God began showing me my purpose again. I was to be a bridge that would connect people to *His* purpose for their lives. I would be a conduit to bring people out of prison, and to connect them with society.

What God Told Me

God asked me, *"Can these bones live?"* This was in reference to a familiar story in the Bible where God was speaking to the prophet Ezekiel in *The Valley of the Dry Bones* (Ezekiel 37). This was a miracle story where God was instructing Ezekiel on how to, basically, make dead things live again. "... and he brought me out in the Spirit of the LORD and set me down in the middle of the valley; it was full of bones. *2* And he led me around among them, and behold, there were very many on the surface of the valley, and behold, they were very dry. *3* And he said to me, "Son of man, *can these bones live?"*

Just as I knew Ezekiel's response in the story, I too said, "You know!" In the text, God told Ezekiel to "prophesy" over the bones. The Lord was telling me, "Speak life to them [the men in prison]." He said, "Speak the 'four winds' to come and speak life to them." The first part I understood. Who were the "four winds?"

God was inspiring me to raise up Reentry Life Coaches; to gather people who would come and speak life to those in prison. Then, He directed me to read the first two verses of Jeremiah 33:1. It says, *"The Spirit of the Lord came to Jeramiah the second time as he was locked up in the courtyard of the prison."* Well, I was locked up. It's amazing how God can speak to us through different parts of His Word at just the right season of our lives.

God then told me, *"I have ordained this, that you will never be ashamed of it."* He said, *"You will call on me. I will answer and show you great and mighty things that you know not of."* God has been true to His Word.

God Was Training Me for His Purpose

To get to know a place I "didn't know of," I had to go behind the walls to learn it. I had to eat with them, work with them, be in the same dorm, and sleep where they slept. I had to experience how people treat them because I was treated the same way. You could be a company president, a drug dealer, or a murderer, you are treated the same there. God was training me for my purpose. We can counsel, coach, teach, and minister to people quite successfully. But when you've been there, done that, and walked a mile in someone's shoes, then you truly understand them. You develop empathy, not just sympathy.

I Changed My Attitude

That's when I started changing my attitude, shifting my thoughts. If God had ordained me to this ministry, I needed to be there to serve them. I was with people all around me who were in despair and didn't have the opportunities, education, or business experience that I had.

After three months of sulking (and a "no" to my appeal), I opened my heart to receive God's explanation and instruction. His purpose for my life hadn't changed. God still called me to serve lost souls, but for a time, He wanted me to reach the least of the least, the most broken and downtrodden of them all. I was doing mission work; but instead of some overseas country it was in the federal prison system.

I Connected with the Men by Shining Their Boots

I prayed to find a way to connect with the men on a more personal level and was given the inspiration to kneel at the feet of each man as I shined his boots. Along with our "khakis," black boots are part of the prison vestment. We were expected to look sharp, especially during visitation. Our clothes should be pressed and starched, and our boots shined so that we "looked" like we were well-cared for. If an inmate's boots were dirty or his clothes wrinkled, he might be denied his visitation, and no one wanted that!

To accomplish the goal of connecting personally with those I served, I required their feet to be in the boots when I cleaned them. This allowed me 15-20 minutes to talk and get to know each "client" (the service was always free, and I bought the shoe polish from the commissary out of my measly monthly earnings). I had a chair set up in my cubicle where the men would sit. I served 2-3 men a day and very soon, like a barber shop, my "shoeshine stand" became the place to hang out and visit.

Our Prison Bully was Named Bones

The stereotype of prison bullies is true, at least from my experience. We had a six-foot-four inmate who was the doppelganger of Dwayne Johnson, "The Rock." His presence was intimidating, and his silence was loaded with threatening danger. He was only known as "Bones;" the nickname clearly not coming from his muscular physique. The source of his name was only grounded in rumor as some were certain the length of his sentence had been shortened because he led detectives to where "the bones were buried." As sensational and widespread as that explanation was, others argued it was because he could literally break bones with his bare hands.

No one knew the truth, not even the henchmen who shadowed him. They were just as terrified by his menacing silence as the rest of us, as the mere motion of his hand could seemingly signal the life-or-death fate of a gladiator. No one wanted Bone's attention, not even his followers. I was the exception. I wanted to connect with him. I don't know if it was the competitor in me that wanted to conquer the Goliath to my David, or because I knew that if I could get to him, I would have the credit to reach many more men. Whatever the reason, the person I wanted in my shoeshine chair the most was Bones.

One day he walked up to my cubicle and demanded I clean his boots by slamming them down in front of me. I informed Bones that I would be happy to shine his boots, but he would have to be in them. In response, Bones brusquely pulled up the chair and sat stiffly, hands placed on his tree-trunk-thighs with fingers in a flexed extension as a display of noncompliance.

He was sitting but wasn't going to relax. Bones looked

straight ahead, past me, refusing to meet my eyes. Ten

minutes of shining his boots passed, then Bones finally

spoke, "So what's your story? You don't look like you

belong here." I lifted my eyes to meet him, as Bones finally

looked down to acknowledge my existence. I grinned,

thinking, *"When I'm done telling my story, you're going to have*

the shiniest pair of boots in the prison."

Chapter 10: My Story

The Tale of My Life and Trial

I began telling Bones my story. It was the first time telling someone "On the inside" my story. "After I graduated from college with a degree in Business Computer Information Systems, I started a computer accounting firm, *Robbins and Associates*, right down the street from Oral Roberts University in Tulsa, Oklahoma. I wasn't trying to go into accounting, but I needed to earn money to continue my studies. I just wanted to pastor, but the business became highly successful, and I eventually had five office locations.

"I started telling Bones personal information like, "While in seminary I met my wife, Kim; we dated for about a year, then got married. We talked a lot about ministry and had similar vision regarding the Church and the people of God.

We began planning a future in ministry."

Already Bone's expression began to soften as he listened to me share our plans to move to Atlanta, Georgia after graduation to start a church. "After moving to Atlanta and having our first child, we planted the church. We celebrated as our congregation and family were growing, and the accounting business expanded into five locations, with an employee operating each office. When we moved to Georgia, we considered closing the office in Tulsa, Oklahoma.

Kim had already suggested that as we made the move to Georgia. A good friend of mine was operating the Tulsa office and I didn't want him to lose his job and his family to lose their income. Initially, I hired him because he had lost his previous job after taking the company car out of town when he wasn't supposed to; basically, he had lost his employment because of a character issue.

As a good friend, I wanted to help and empower him, so I chose to trust him and give him an opportunity to work for me and be able to continue to support his family. The decision to help this friend out by keeping him on as an employee was a "good" thing, but not a God thing. We aren't supposed to do good things, we are to do "God things."

I continued my story.

"Leaving that office open, his character failed him again, and I didn't know about it until much later. He was using my company to help people with their tax deductions. He was heavy on the write-offs for about 17 businesses over a two-year span. It turned out that those businesses were also not legitimate. He also had checks that he deposited in his personal account instead of the corporate account. I discovered the problem when I came to do an audit, but by then the IRS had already issued indictments for 65 counts of false tax returns."

"Ouch," I heard him whisper.

"Since he had been doing this under the company that I owned, the IRS looked at me as the 'Big Fish' they needed to catch. There was a young prosecutor trying to make a name for herself, wanting a big conviction. She also needed to justify why she was investigating my employee. Basically, the government spent a half million dollars of taxpayers' money to bring about a conviction for tax returns owing just $87,000. I was brought into the case through conspiracy and tied into 15 of the 65 counts.

I was indicted for conspiracy, so I hired one of the best tax accounting lawyers. There were only eight major ones throughout the U.S., and he was one of them. We prepared for about a year. I agreed to a $60,000 cost to have him represent me while my co-defendant had a court-appointed attorney.

On a speaker phone, when talking to my lawyer and not knowing I was in the room, the prosecutor said, *'We aren't going to give Mr. Robbins a plea deal, because he probably won't lie on himself.'* My attorney agreed and said I wouldn't take it anyway, and that I wanted to go to trial to prove my innocence. Even after being advised that most people lose going to trial against the United States and that they lose in court 85% percent of the time, and 90% of lawsuits involving the government are plea deals that never go to trial, I ran the risk of getting a 15-year sentence. But I wanted to prove my innocence and was determined to clear my name. I didn't know anything about the system because I had never been in trouble with the law.

On the first day of the trial, tax returns and witnesses were brought to the court. The witnesses didn't know me, couldn't identify me, but they recognized my co-defendant. My name and signatures were not on the returns.

I had never met the people or seen these documents. The judge got irritated. He demanded to know, *'Why are we having this trial against Mr. Robbins if his name wasn't even on the documents?'* At first, I saw triumph. There was no evidence against me. But on the third day, suddenly, a tax return showed up with my company stamp on it.

I found out that my stamp had been given over to the prosecution as part of the evidence, so they stamped the tax return with my signature. However, they couldn't stamp the copy in my possession. There are long numbers on every document and mine was a copy of theirs, but without the stamp. I pointed it out to my lawyer, 'Look, this one doesn't have the stamp on it, but the one in trial has been stamped.' My lawyer said, 'We've got them now! Someone's going to prison, but it won't be you!"

At cross-examination, my attorney held up our document, without the stamp on it and their document with the stamp on it. Six prosecutors all visibly slid down in their seats. The judge must have seen this because he ended the proceedings. It was in the middle of the day, and he didn't stop it for lunch, not for an hour, not a 30-minute recess, but he concluded it for the day. As I was walking out of the courtroom, I noticed the prosecutors were in a frantic huddle. They looked at me and stopped talking, knowing they had not done the right thing. I was feeling elated that this nightmare was about to end.

The next day, my lawyer informed me that he had five years of tax returns he didn't file. I thought, 'Now, why would he mention that now, after we've been preparing for a year?' I think he wanted me to fire him on the spot and get him removed from my case, but we had already invested $30,000 into him and this trial appeared to be over.

I didn't think this information he shared about his taxes would be used as leverage against me. My attorney's attitude soon changed. His boldness to deal with them on my behalf began to wane. They also changed my co-defendant's court-appointed attorney to a formerly retired prosecutor. They needed my employee to be found innocent to not find me in conspiracy. They knew I had done no wrong. The prosecutors wanted to convict me of 15 counts, but not conspiracy of all 65 counts so that I wouldn't get the full 15 years. They used a guilty man as leverage against me, the person they really wanted to convict. It was his word against mine. He took the stand and said he didn't do any of the tax returns. I slid a note to my attorney and said "He's lying. Put me on the stand." But my lawyer refused to call me to testify of my innocence.

I believe that was his agreement with the prosecution, to avoid prison time himself for his tax evasion. In other words, not allowing me to take the stand prevented me from testifying to my innocence. At the opening of the trial, my attorney had said, 'You will hear from my client that he didn't do those tax returns and we can prove he didn't.' But I never got the chance to testify. In fact, he told the jury, in his closing remarks, that the prosecutors had won this case. Who would say something like that if they hadn't already sold you out?

In the end, all he did was call a few character witnesses, with the sole purpose of determining what kind of sentence I would be given, trying to ensure it wasn't too bad. While this was happening, I was going into a depression right there in the courtroom. I felt like Daniel in the lion's den. Everyone was against me, and I was watching my life go down.

After preaching in the pulpit, helping people, pastoring a church, counseling, baptizing, and blessing babies, I found myself in a courtroom about to be convicted of fraud and, most likely, go to prison. I was going from the pulpit to the pit, when I was used to being the one pulling people out of the pit.

It took the jury the entire weekend to come to a verdict. It was difficult because a few obviously knew something was wrong. But they were given these rules, if this person fits the criteria, you must find them guilty. If they aren't innocent without a shadow of a doubt, you must find them guilty. Whether you think they are innocent or not, if it fits this criterion, you must find the person guilty. I saw the ways some of the jurors were looking at me as they came out to deliver the verdict. A few of the women were even crying in the jury. They knew they were getting ready to convict an innocent man and had no control over it.

I was ordered to stand to hear the verdict. I was found guilty of 15 counts of preparation of false tax returns. It was a paper crime; no money was received by me. The tax dollars were reclaimed; the government got 100% of their money back. They found me guilty and my co-defendant innocent on all charges.

When I came back later for the sentencing, I learned that the prosecutor on my case couldn't make it because her mother had died and the funeral was that day. Prosecutors like to come to sentencing. They want you to get the maximum and then celebrate that they put you away.

Well, this "Big Fish" had a wife and three small children, seven, five and two years old. I had shown them the pictures during the trial so they could understand the implications of this injustice. They were hurting my wife and these three beautiful children.

The judge feigned compassion and said, 'Since you have been a law-abiding upstanding citizen until now, I'm just going to give you three and a half years. Get your business in order and in 21 days report to the Federal Prison Camp in Atlanta Georgia.' At least he allowed me to be closer to my family in Atlanta, so they didn't have to travel so far to see me."

While looking at Bones, I said, "Well, that's my story!"

I saw an expression on his face I had never seen before compassion. "Awww, Pastor Lee," he said, shaking his head vigorously, "You got done wrong!"

Chapter 11: Working for Good

Once I shifted my thoughts, changed my attitude about my situation, and found a way to connect with the men by shining their boots, I was determined to leave a legacy in this place. I realized that I was innocent, but not sinless; and that God had a plan and purpose for my life and this time in prison. As I worked to connect with the men, I began to see their needs and how I could help by giving them purpose in the present and creating hope for their future.

I was set on helping them change their lives, not just by becoming a follower of Christ but I wanted them to leave there and go make a difference in their family, their community, and the world. I accepted that God wanted me to do prison time to use my prison experience as a pulpit to help others. I remembered what my daughter had said about working for God.

"I'm called here," I thought. "So, let me really get to work!"

This is how you make use of your pain. You must see the narrative differently. Look into the situations of your life and see, not what the outcome could have been or how you wished it would have happened differently, but what is your take-away? How can this pain be used for a greater purpose to help someone else?

The PATH Program (Purpose Achieved Through Him)

I began developing a program called *The PATH* which organized some of the more talented inmates into coaches to help the younger prisoners in various areas of their lives. I used the acronym *"F.R.E.S.H. L.I.F.E."* which stood for Financial, Relationships, Education, Spiritual, Health, Legal, Investments, Fitness, and Entrepreneurship/Employment. These were the areas on which *The PATH* program focused.

In our Federal Prison, there were people from all walks of life who could effectively teach these subjects. I recruited a CPA who helped the younger inmates with financial planning while ex-counselors and even ex-NFL players addressed health and fitness. Ex-politicians and professionals of all types contributed their expertise, and *The PATH* program became an active way to help prisoners prepare for reentry.

The classes met once a week for three months, after which we held a graduation.

Although official classes met weekly, the coaches took such an interest in their students they met with them between classes. They helped them with homework and developing their reentry plans in writing. Everyone had a common goal… to ensure that once released, no one came back!

Another benefit of the program became apparent. The coaches turned into more than teachers for the younger inmates. They began to fill voids, serving as friends, fathers, mentors, and counselors. As the self-esteem of the young ones grew, so did the joy and purpose of those who coached. I watched everyone in the program become ALIVE before my eyes. Even Bones joined. It was amazing to discover his hidden personality, once he found a place among the program leaders.

His once quiet, intimidating demeanor turned into someone talkative and expressive. Of all the transformations I saw, Bones was the biggest change. He became friendly and helpful, thanking me regularly for showing him how to "make something out of his prison life."

As a result of my relationship with Bones, I felt comfortable enough around him to finally ask, "Why do they call you Bones?" He looked both ways, pulled me aside and said, "I'll tell you, but you can't tell nobody!" I agreed. Then he whispered, "When I was a kid, I loved Star Trek. I wanted to grow up to be a medical doctor, just like the guy on The Enterprise. My family made fun of me and called me 'Bones.' I've had that name ever since."

It was a good lesson for me. We just never know what genuine people are hidden behind insecurities, making them appear mean or aloof. Finally breaking through to this revived man, I remembered the question God asked me straight from the Bible when I first arrived, "Can these bones live?" As I watched him talking, laughing, and smiling with his students, I said, "Yes Lord, Bones has come to life!"

My Prison Job

The job I was assigned in prison became the perfect opportunity to help those coming in and leaving the camp population. I worked in R & D. R & D stood for Receiving and Discharge; but I referred to it as "Redeemed and Delivered." This role was exclusively assigned to individuals who had earned the trust of the officers and administrators. They closely observed my behavior within the compound and concluded that I could be relied upon to handle the responsibilities of the R & D position.

I was the first-person people would see when they entered the camp and the last one to see them on their way back into society. I helped them get their linens, their green "suits," and any other provisions given by the camp for their stay. I explained the rules and got them prepared for their new accommodation.

Prison Privileges

Because of the job I had, the reputation I had developed, and the pastoring I was doing in prison, I was favored with certain "privileges." These blessings came mostly through my fellow inmates. Sometimes, while headed to "chow," the line of green sea would open up to let me through so that I could be the first person in line to get food. Other times, some residents would have my food fixed just the way I wanted it and bring it to me. I didn't have any extra authority in prison, but the residents took it upon themselves to be a blessing to me.

Prison Became My Congregation

As I mentioned earlier, before entering the Federal Prison Camp I was pastoring a church with my wife. We had established its foundation and structure, built infrastructure, and grew the congregation. But my current circumstances had taken me from that role. Now, the prison was becoming my "church." This was now my pulpit from which I would share God's love and His Word to reach others for Christ. I had a new congregation and would eventually see well over 300 people give their life to Jesus. I began to understand that it was partially my fault that I was in prison. I had made some bad choices. No, I didn't commit the crime for which I was accused.

However, I had hired a guy whose character had come into question and who abused his responsibilities to my company. I had forgiven everyone involved in my case: the judge, who railroaded me, the prosecutor, who covered the truth with a lie just to win, and my co-defendant, a fellow believer who chose the love of money and the testimony of a lie. But now God was turning all of this in my favor. I was helping others forgive themselves, their situations and those involved in them, and ask for forgiveness so they might have eternal life.

Our church services in the camp were powerful. We had people who provided instruments so we could have a full band. The guys used their talents of song and music to usher us into God's presence. We saw Muslims, Atheists, and others come to know the Lord personally. I also used this time in prison to "evangelize." I had always either led the local church evangelism team or participated in one, as well as witnessing others by myself. I was used to all types of people and used my Evangelism Explosion information and expertise to win others to Christ. In prison you kind of have a "captive audience." The opportunities were ongoing. I sometimes would ask God to give me a word for someone. I would write them down on notecards and share them with the people when the time was right.

One such example was when I wrote down the age and date about a pain that occurred to a fellow inmate. I later shared this with him. At first, he said that nothing traumatic had happened to him at the age of 15 (which is what I had written) but then after a little thought, he realized that he saw his dad get stabbed and die at that time. God then spoke more into his life. This is referred to in scripture as a "word of knowledge." I did not know his situation, but God did. And the Lord wanted to minister to him but needed to first get his attention that He's real and that He cares about the things that bring us pain.

There are so many stories and incredible things that happened during my time in the camp that the testimonies themselves could fill an entire book. I can't possibly share them all here. However, there is one powerful story that I must mention. It is a story of faith, the power of God, and the agreement of believers.

Remember, earlier in my life story when my best friend died in my arms, and I said that another would come to life again? Well, this is that time. I was having Bible Study with about 10 other believers one day in the chapel. We, the church, had been having revival services in the camp. We were fasting from prison food (which wasn't all that difficult since it was so bad) and spending a lot of time in prayer and the Word. God was moving powerfully in these services. One day, I think it was a Saturday, but I can't recall exactly, I was sharing the Word with some new believers. During this time, one of the officers asked two inmates to carry a man on a stretcher over to us because he did not have a pulse. The officer said, "Robbins, I need you to pray for this guy before I report his death." This man had died on the officer's watch, and he wanted to try everything he could to help the man before he turned it over to his superiors.

I told those who were with me, "If you don't have faith to believe this man can be raised from the dead, leave now." About half or more left! It was me and about two or three other guys who remained. I wasn't so sure myself really, but I was determined to stand in faith. I knew God

could do it. But would he use us? We laid our hands on the

man, and I commanded that his life return to his body. He

took a breath and opened his eyes and asked, "Where am

I?" I said, "You're still in prison." He said, "Dern, Robbins

you should have left me dead." One would die in my arms

from a bullet intended for me, but with my hands I would

feel the breath of another return to him by faith in the

God we serve.

SECTION 3

TIME TO TAKE PURPOSE OUTSIDE THE WIRE

Chapter 12: Time to Go

It Was Time to Go!

When the time for my release approached, I began preparing the "church behind walls" for the impending transition. I spent my last month training those who would assume the leadership role(s) in which I had been operating. I had been the primary minister in our chapel services, and I needed to pass the baton.

The next pastor in line was Bob Bedford and it brought me tremendous satisfaction to see him step into his new role, especially as the church organically grew to love and see him as their leader. His story, like mine, was an unfortunate error. However, he was positive, and a strong believer and I knew the men would be well-equipped in my absence. We had a special ceremony the Sunday night before I left. It was an anointed service.

It was a blessing to watch the men accept Bob as their new minister.

While the goodbyes began weeks ahead, the emotions of the night before my departure ran high. I had a checklist on what items I needed to return to the prison, and I set these items aside. I then began giving away the rest of my possessions. There were some inmates who had been so destitute they couldn't even buy necessities from the commissary (keep in mind, people needed personal hygiene items too). I was able to pass on things that filled their wishes right down to the very shoes on my feet.

I gave away everything, including my books and bibles. While my friends may have been sad to see me go, they were ecstatic about these gifts they received! As I walked through the dormitory, I repeatedly heard, "Thank you, thank you, thank you!" It was as if it were Christmas Eve, and I was Santa Clause.

I even let out a few "Ho, Ho, Ho's" to play up the cheerfulness in the room. It was *my* Christmas Eve, the night before freedom, and the presents were parting expressions of love and "God be with you till we meet again."

The Happiest Meal Ever

The day had finally arrived! My wife was there right on time the next morning to pick me up, along with the kids, her sister, brother, and my niece. They had driven down from North Carolina to greet me "at the door." This was a welcome surprise!

"Where would you like to eat after all this time and that wonderful prison food?" they asked. You might think I shouted, "Steak!" But what I missed most, what I hadn't eaten in years, was a good old-fashioned McDonald's hamburger! So off we went to the *Golden Arches* and my family watched as I devoured my Big Mac with the stupid jingle running through my mind, "two all-beef patties, special sauce, lettuce, cheese, pickles, onions, on a sesame seed bun!"

I felt exactly like a kid finally getting out of school for the summer. I could have jumped into the playground ball pit with the rest of the kids, I felt so giddy. Instead, we had a captivating free-world conversation, which is very different from the topics in prison. But then it was over, and it was time to go to my next stop for another four months.

Reporting to the Transition Center

Because of *The Second Chance Act*, I was released from prison six months early but still had to live under supervision at this location, away from my family and without full freedom. The transition center had curfews and certain items were considered contraband, such as cell phones, which could only be used during the day and had to be checked in at night.

I suspect one of the reasons they did this was because they didn't want pictures taken of the conditions there. It may be called a transition center, but it wasn't much better than prison accommodations. I spent four months in this halfway house, even though I had a loving family and home waiting for me, all for a paper crime with no money lost and no victims. While in this place, I was required to get a job. They want to make sure you get gainful employment before they let you go completely. The problem is no one wants to hire someone with a criminal background. I might as well have committed an act of treason or something. This is another reason I started other services to help those coming out of prison. I had a master's level education, but I couldn't even get a job at a fast-food establishment. I couldn't even get an interview! It was humiliating. As soon as they saw "ex-felon" on my application, it went straight into the trash bin.

My "job" initially was traveling to the Department of Labor, two hours daily, in an attempt to find employment. I must have applied to over 100 places. Still, nothing. My time in the transitional center was like the prison experience, only shorter. I found a way to connect with those in leadership and was allowed opportunities, such as organizing a Christmas program. There I had the opportunity to be the keynote speaker. God gave me favor everywhere I went, even in places where people had no privileges. I believe He showed me such favor because I wasn't there to be corrected but to serve a mission. I was to lay my life down, for a time, for those in prison.

In addition to speaking, I became a mentor. It helped tremendously being in that role. I used the "coach approach" in all our meetings. What I started in prison I was able to continue at the transition center.

Chapter 13: Returning Home

When I returned home, I was under supervised release. An officer would come to our house at least once a month to gauge my progress. The person who visited me knew I was a pastor. He felt uncomfortable checking up on me because he knew I wasn't a risk. What might I do, run down the street, and do someone's taxes? Seriously. The blanket of the penal system does not discriminate against the crime committed (or supposedly committed) when it comes to supervised release.

He had to go through the process of asking the questions even though he knew it was unnecessary. He didn't stay very long. He knew I wasn't going to be a problem. We had good, Godly conversations and then he'd leave. Before long, the officer asked his superiors to allow me to be removed from supervision early. They approved it and changed our visits to calls.

I also wore an ankle monitor for a time. If they called to check on you, you'd better answer the phone, or you could get locked up again. One time they called about two o'clock in the morning. I leaped out of the bed, half asleep, struggling to get my feet under me, running into walls to get to the phone before they hung up. We had a phone in our bedroom, but it was not a landline phone and It had to be a landline. That phone was in the kitchen and that is why I was sprinting, fearing I might miss the call and be sent back to prison. It's easier than you think to get carted off and returned to the place from which you were just freed (I could preach a message right there).

I was breathing hard after running to the phone. They asked if I was alright and questioned if I had just run from down the street. I said, "It's 2 a.m.! I had to wake up first." I wanted to spout a lot more than that, but you must be on guard; so, all I could do was pray for those people. They are taught to be mean.

Family First

The direction I received from God when I finally went home was to put the family first. I was in a unique situation. Kim had been in the role of both mom and dad for three and a half years. Before, when the kids wanted something, they would ask either or both of us, but now they just go to mom. A returning citizen needs to understand that you "get in where you fit in." You can't suddenly break up the established structure and jump into being the authoritative figure. When the kids visited me in prison, I didn't get on them about things because I wanted visitation to be pleasant; so, when I came home, I had to allow time for them to adjust to me being the father figure again.

It was my goal to accommodate, assist and be available, and not as a disciplinarian; I didn't want to be the correction officer at the house! Many officers get behind the badge and abuse their authority over others.

They don't understand authority and often misuse it. Authority is a responsibility to serve others. I learned quickly that I needed to be a servant-leader in my home. Without that realization, it can be difficult for people to transition back from prison. We had been happy-go-lucky for those years during our visits, in our "Hulk Time" and Kim helped me see that I needed to slowly step back into my role. Previously, I thought my family couldn't get by without me, but they had.

My family was resilient, and not only could they make it, but they also did! Realizing my family had survived without me caused a variety of emotions. I felt blessed that they had made it, but also wondered where I fit in now. I began by serving them the best I could, doing household chores like the laundry, dishes, etc.

Because of my house arrest, I wasn't able to travel with my family when they went on vacation to grandma and grandpas, so I held down the fort and took care of the dog.

I wanted them to have fun and not stop their plans.

Our Dog Max

You may wonder why I'm talking about our dog. But this was another painful point in my life which, while it may not have been avoided, could have gone much more smoothly if I hadn't still been in this situation.

Our 14-year-old dog, Max, had been with us since Kim and I were married. He was our first kid! While the family was out of town, he became sick, not eating, and wandering away when I let him out. Kim didn't take him with her as she usually did because he had started pacing a lot and his eyesight was getting bad. We thought at first, he was just having separation anxiety from her when I told her he wasn't eating.

But as it continued, we believed he had a blockage in his stomach or something. Kim had to deal with the emotion of leaving him in that state for two weeks. SinceI was locked down at home, I couldn't take him anywhere but had to wait until the family returned.

If we had been able to take him to the vet, he probably would have lived a few years longer. He basically spent two weeks dying of starvation because he couldn't eat or drink anything. It was tough to watch. We simply didn't have the finances because I had been away and unable to provide vet care for Max. Not only that, but we also had one vehicle at the time and Kim was about seven hours away with the kids for two weeks. And, of course, I was still on house arrest and not allowed to travel outside the state.

When they returned Max was barely alive. It's as if he had waited for Kim to get home so he could say goodbye. Kim groomed him up as best she could so we could take him to be euthanized. We could only afford the $20 to euthanize him. For the vet to do it would still have cost too much. We called but it just wasn't within our budget. She had already felt bad because she couldn't attend to his needs since she had three young kids she had to raise with few breaks and no help.

As it happened, my house arrest ended right after they got back. That's right, we were only two weeks away from full freedom and I was unable to travel for vacation with my family and unable to help my dog with what ailed him. Sometimes, it's the seemingly less important things that can become the most important.

Since I had just gotten off house arrest, I was able to be the one to take him to the pound to be put down. Ironically, it was my first drive for freedom and resulted in locking up my dog in a kennel until it was time to leave this world, with his eyes telling me he knew this was the end. He was the only one there, all alone behind wires, awaiting the *Green Mile.*

I had the biggest cry of my life leaving that place. I thought I was strong in prison but being the one to say the final goodbye to our little dog after 14 years, and sparing my family the pain, was almost more than my heart could bear. I cried all the way home.

I didn't have shackles on my ankles anymore and was able to start really doing some meaningful things for my family.

After Supervised Release

When I was taken off the supervised release, I got a job with Campus Crusade for Christ. I went into high schools after school let out for the day, bringing pizza, and facilitating a meeting for them to share their testimonies and life stories. They did all the teaching and worship, inviting students to attend. I had to fundraise to pay for my employment with them and the food I brought.

This experience of struggling to find gainful employment inspired me to start reentry support programs. I also got active with churches, men's ministries, government services, returning citizens, and starting businesses to serve people.

Chapter 14: How Pain Pushed Me into Purpose

I found His purpose for my life ... connecting people coming out of prison, bridging police officers with the public, bridging races, and building bridges in the community.

Understanding the pain that has happened in your life and how to allow it to push you to purpose can be a process. First, we have the tendency to bury our pain and trauma in life because it hurts so bad. And, if we fail to harness the power of our pain, it may silently inflict punishment upon us. However, if we leverage our pain, we become equipped to recognize and console others with the same solace that we ourselves have received ... (2 Cor. 1 : 3 - 7) This is how pain pushes us into purpose.

Kingdom Life Church

While I was still incarcerated, Kim and I began working on our next church plant. I would send her some info, she would create curriculum and infrastructure, and we would make plans on when and how to start this endeavor. Our heart was to preach the Word of the Kingdom, so we called the church Kingdom Life Church. We had great vision and passion for teaching these powerful principles of God's Kingdom. Kingdom Life Church would focus our outreach efforts on returning citizens.

We began to be appreciated by people incarcerated in prison as well as with prison officials. We found people in the Body of Christ who also had a heart for the incarcerated and teamed up with them to minister to this marginalized and disenfranchised group.

I, and others working with me, would go to transitional centers and preach. We soon started bringing vans of people, and carpooling some, from the transitional center to the church. The prison system gave us permission and we were more than eager to assist. We even had one sweet lady we called Mom May who absolutely loved prison ministry and opened her home for lots of home cooked food and fellowship with the guys after church.

About 80% of the people in our congregation on any given Sunday ended up being former or currently incarcerated individuals. It was awesome because it was also a place for families to have an opportunity to come together during their loved one's time at the Transitional Center. We called it family reunification in church. It was successful until someone had to mess it up. Though it wasn't during our church service per se, one of the guys decided to escape one Sunday.

We could no longer continue the program.

We quickly realized we couldn't put all our eggs in the same basket. A person can make one decision and three fourths of the congregation would be gone. Rather than transition, because we had so many working parts and were still operating as Kingdom Life Church inside the Transition Center, we decided to close Kingdom Life Church on the outside and start another church plant. This time we would do things differently. Our new church was, and still is, called The Source Church.

After running Kingdom Life inside the center for a few years we transitioned that as well into one of our "house churches." The eagerness to be a blessing to the guys but realizing we had to have more help and structure in place to better serve them was a learning experience.

Our First Reentry Home

Five years after I had returned from prison, I opened our first reentry home. We began focusing on helping citizens coming home from prison. I started volunteering for Prison Fellowship, the largest prison ministry organization in the country, and it allowed me to go back inside, mentor people, and then invite them to continue with our reentry support when they were released. The men in prison identified with me since I had once been where they were now. It gave me prison credibility, so they listened. I made sure everyone I helped had a life coach, housing, food, and clothing. The resources I needed to accomplish all these services came from the church I was pastoring.

Churches and Returning Citizens

It's vitally important for churches to get involved with helping returning citizens rebuild their lives, and to see them as neighbors, not felons. I started the reentry services through my church, knowing other churches would come along after seeing how it's done. As mentioned earlier, we've learned by experience. We know where the holes are, we understand the issues an outreach ministry like this may have, and we can help churches establish a solid base for transforming lives from the pit to His purpose for their lives.

Georgia Prison Reentry Initiative (PRI)

My opportunity to help with reentry increased when I was given the position as the Community Coordinator for the State of Georgia. I worked for the Governor's office as part of the Georgia Prison Reentry (PRI) Initiative. This was funded by the federal government's Second Chance Act at a level of $6 million dollars.

This funding helped the state hire a person like me to help make the prison reentry initiative successful.

Given my criminal record, I couldn't understand how I got that job. I was upfront and honest, but the interviewers said they saw nothing in my record. I was curious, so I investigated it. I discovered that my records had been sealed. My trial had been so corrupt, they didn't want any other lawyer to have access to it and possibly sue for how heavily I was railroaded.

In this position with the State of Georgia, 11 years after this whole thing began, I could see how providential my life had been. I had to go through what I did in prison to learn, but in the end, my record was clean. Nothing was missing or broken in my life. God said I'd never be ashamed, and I truly have never been embarrassed to share my testimony because of how God has used it for so many things and in so many ways.

I wouldn't be where I am today if I had not gone through this prison experience, working hard to develop my skills in these areas and accepting this direction as a ministry and calling. God rewards His servants, and He has genuinely rewarded me. I didn't have to chase money; I just needed to find His purpose for my life.

Georgia Governor Deal supported the Georgia Prison Reentry Initiative (PRI) and hired me as the only community coordinator for Gwinnett County. My responsibility was to get resources for returning citizens and to expand resource capacities. I did work for the Department of Community Supervision (DCS) aka probation and parole.

The State of Georgia was funded for a pilot program where they hired about 17 people like me. The program was successful because it funded community coordinators (developing resources and relationships for the people coming out), in reach coordinators (who worked in prisons), and housing coordinators (housing was the biggest problem because people getting out of prison had such difficulty finding a place to live).

With a lot of collaboration, we helped reduce the prison recidivism rate in the state of Georgia. We worked to reduce the negative impact of the silos (when individuals or organizations isolate themselves from others, resulting in limited interaction and a lack of collaboration or shared experience) which makes it hard for returning citizens. I was proud to be a part of this program.

I also helped sponsor reentry resource rallies. These rallies brought all the resources together in one place and we got the word out for returning citizens to go to these rallies. We also created reentry hubs in churches and faith-based organizations. This helped the returning citizens and resources when the rallies were over.

One of the leaders in the program, Tony Lowden, was selected to a newly created position, Czar of Reentry, by former President Trump, to continue the work on a larger scale with the hope of expanding the model nationwide.

S.A.F.E. Staffing

After four years, I resigned from my state job so I could focus more on specific resources for the reentry population. I started S.A.F.E. Staffing. It is a three-tiered staffing company that partners with state agencies to help returning citizens get jobs and develop careers through education and certifications.

Some of the people we serve even go on to become successful entrepreneurs. It was a difficult decision to resign from my position with the government. I had a good employment package with a decent salary and medical plan. It didn't necessarily look like a good financial move, but I felt directed to focus on that aspect of reentry and I wanted to avoid any conflict of interest.

When the Coronavirus hit, the state cut the funding for the position I had held. In fact, many of the Community Coordinators were let go. If I had not listened to the voice of God, I would have been unemployed and not be in the position with S.A.F.E. Staffing.

The Source Church

I mentioned earlier that we planted another church called The Source Church. We started this church in May of 2014 with the idea that we're going to be community driven, not just prison driven. We began reaching out to our immediate community without putting an emphasis on prison reentry. We had come to learn that people, even in the church, are often afraid to attend if they know criminals were also in attendance. Our goal now has become to raise people up as leaders.

We shifted our services, and we began online services in early 2020. What timing! Shortly thereafter the pandemic hit. We were already prepared. We still do online service, but we are also building "house churches" to meet community needs on a more personal level. If you would like more information about The Source Church Unlimited, please visit our website at www.thesource.church.

My Wife, Kim

Kim played a significant role in establishing Christian education within The Source Church and the churches before it. Graduating with honors from Oral Roberts University with a Master of Divinity degree, she possesses a strong theological foundation. Her contributions encompass the development of Christian education materials, curricula, and training programs, catering to both adults and youth.

Kim's versatility also allowed her to have excelled in constructing ministry infrastructures, frameworks, and resource materials. Her multifaceted talents also encompass the creation of most of our ministry and business websites. Additionally, she skillfully led our worship team and served as the worship leader.

Moreover, Kim demonstrated exceptional leadership, co-pastoring alongside me and even leading the church independently in my absence. Beyond our shared ministry, she has cultivated her own independent ministry known as Kim Robbins Ministries. Through this itinerant ministry, she passionately speaks at churches, conferences, seminars, panels, and more. For more information about Kim and the ministry the Lord has assigned her, please visit www.kimrobbins.org.

Life Empowerment Enterprises

I established Life Empowerment Enterprises as an incorporated for-profit organization to serve people who were getting out early because of the Second Chance Act. Life Empowerment Enterprises is a life coach certification company that helps returning citizens to safely and successfully return to their community. It has now become the household name all over the country for life coaching specifically targeting returning citizens.

Our clientele are formerly incarcerated individuals. By becoming equipped with tools and gaining their certification, they can effectively coach other returning citizens. These life coaches have automatic credibility because they have been incarcerated themselves. The life coaches receive a Coach's Life Guide and are a bridge for those who come out of prison.

They learn about coaching for finding community resources, housing, healthcare, and so forth. Not all of our coaches have served time, but they all have a heart and passion in the area of reentry.

Life Empowerment Enterprises uses a powerful reentry case management software called the Pokket (owed and created by Acivilate) where we keep up with our clients, their goals, community and governmental resources, and coaching sessions. It is very secure with usernames and passwords. It is a great tool for the returning citizen and our coaches.

The coaches are trained to ask good questions and are expected to be good listeners. They guide the process as an adult relationship, an adult talking to an adult. Our philosophy is not to communicate like an adult talking to a child.

We don't want to tell this population of returning citizens what to do because they've already been told what to do all their lives. We want to be part of their life. Help them plan their life success. We help people navigate, which means we are life navigators. We help people determine their goals, if they need help with that. And once they know their goal(s), we help them navigate to get to that place. It's like having a life GPS.

More than 1000 people from all over the country have earned a life coach certification from Life Empowerment Enterprises. Our clients are individuals and federal, state, and local governments.

My Manifesto

Life empowerment coaching is very close to my heart because it's my way of making disciples. My manifesto is

- Make disciples
- Make heaven their home
- Make an abundant life
- Make God smile with what I do with it
- Make no excuses, only adjustments.

Vital Signs

Vital Signs is part of Life Empowerment Enterprises, though it operates as a 501c3 nonprofit organization. Its main component is to provide housing (a group home) for the returning citizen. We have housing for adults and for juveniles. This is for rehabilitation.

We have housing for juveniles before they are sentenced to a state criminal corrections facility. In other words, a judge can give a young person 18 to 24 years old an opportunity for the group home. This is for prevention. While here, they learn life and job skills.

In our program, the people we serve have six months to a year to get on their feet. They receive a life coach to help them with that process. People can make donations and gifts to the nonprofit to help pay for their program fees. We have also received grants and contributions from global ministries to support our housing goals.

Reentry Transportation Service for Returning Citizens

I am always on the lookout for opportunities to find resources and funding for returning citizens and the wrap-around services we provide (none of which are free). I found one such contest a few years ago. It was a contest for a $25,000 prize with United Way. Unfortunately, I did not win that cash prize for the reentry program.

However, I then discovered that Primerica had a contest for innovative projects. I entered that contest with my innovation for transportation to the reentry population and won $10,000!

Then, since Primerica thought I should have won the United Way contest, they awarded me $15,000 more Now, we receive $25,000 every year from Primerica to fund the project. That is how we initiated our transportation services called UpLift. UpLift provides rides for returning citizens to get to the probation office, their jobs, and any special classes. We provide 1000's of rides each year.

Tackle The Shackles

This is another idea God put on my heart to help prison reform and the reentry process. I founded Tackle the Shackles, a Nation Reentry Coalition, where the goal is to tackle the problems of reentry by getting the star power of NFL players to help bring awareness and attention to it. Many NFL players enjoy helping community organizations and reentry is an often-overlooked opportunity to create lasting change in the lives of others.

I felt people would respect NFL players. These guys have star power, and some have even found themselves facing the justice system. We also like to include military veterans in this vision. We know that some veterans can end up in prison because of PTSD problems. I started by recruiting former NFL players who are used to being out front and brought them on as Ambassadors.

Buddy Curry, who is in the Atlanta Falcons Hall of Fame and was a legendary player for the Falcons from 1980 to 1987 is one of my ambassadors. He wanted to be hands-on with the program and travels with me inside a transition center every week. He became certified by Life Empowerment.

Santos Stevens is another former NFL player who has come on board as an ambassador. Stevens made the very first tackle for the Jacksonville Jaguars franchise over 25 years ago. He is very excited about our goals and program, and he also happens to be in prison ministry.

Mike Barber has also come on board as an Ambassador with Tackle the Shackles. He has already been in prison ministry for years, of course, in connection with Kenneth Copeland who has often gone into prison with him and whom I met while at the Federal Camp when he was visiting someone there.

Tackle The Shackles operates all over the country. I would like to see Tackle the Shackles become the next "United Way" for Reentry. I also started a Tackle the Shackles live streaming podcast. We stream on Facebook and YouTube every Monday night. Buddy Curry is my co-host, and we have a returning citizen share their story, which is often a "rags to riches" story. We created Tackle the Shackles T-shirts and when I'm out meeting people it creates an opportunity to have a conversation about what we are doing. Recently, I met a nationally known sports announcer at a Subway restaurant. He didn't know anything about me or reentry, but he bought my sandwich and wants to know about my dream of having a Fastbreak

Reentry program and involving the NBA and basketball players. I am writing this to remind readers that people want to help. We simply need to ask and show them how.

There are many more things in the works. People want to help, and resources are waiting to be released. When we allow pain to not bring us down but take us into a place where we can help others going through similar life situations, then we can begin to transform our pain and allow God to create a purpose from it.

Documentary

We were set to do a documentary about reentry and some of the things we were doing. But a powerful opportunity came up at the time we began recording. We had a returning citizen, Larry, who came to our Vital Signs reentry home. He had served 42 years in prison, and this was his first week out. The documentary shifted and began to follow Larry on his journey back into society from his long stint behind bars. It is a culture shock after all that time. Once finished, our documentary was called *First Week Out*.

The documentary company that funded the project was Iron light Labs. The documentary has been shown in more than 60 private viewings and has won several awards. Did you know that on average 10,000 people come out ut of prison into the community every week? The documentary company looked at his first week and how successful he had been in the program. Today, Larry has his own house, car, and he's still working at 65 years old. He's doing well!

One of the owners of the documentary company is a personal advisor to me and his company helps us with social media and fundraising. He invites me and Larry to the Nashville Conference every year to celebrate success. He likes to support nonprofit causes and empower their purpose. We are currently working together and researching the possibility of establishing a Tiny Home Village for returning citizens. We want to name it after his late brother, whose last name is Green. We will call it

God's Tiny Green Houses.

Conclusion

Painful Lessons that were Leveraged on Purpose

God said that we can "become a book (epistle) read by all men." *"Pain Pushed Me into Purpose"* is not just about my life story but about how we, with God's help, can turn the pain of our lives into something greater and for the greater good.

Here are 10 lessons to help you leverage pain on purpose:

1. *Peace is not the absence of pain but the presence of purpose.* The source of my pain may not be the same as yours, but God can give you peace in the midst of that pain. People, yourself included, may not even comprehend how you could have peace during your trials. But God can help you find purpose from it. (Philippians 4:7)

2.   *Bad things can happen to well-meaning people but always for a good purpose.* God is good and has great plans for us (Jeremiah 29:11). We may not always be good, but God knows how to work all things together for good (Romans 3:10-12; Romans 8:28)

3.   *Solutions to problems are never solved by theory but through people with lived experiences.* There are simply things that cannot be learned in the classroom or the boardroom. They must be learned through life experiences. Education can be expensive, but you don't always have to pay for it with money. Sometimes it requires the "trial of your faith" (1 Peter 1:7).

4.   *There is a difference between doing good things versus doing "God" things.* Good things may end up being God things, if they are in line with His purpose for our lives; but they are not the same. We often think we are good because we do good things but learning to obey God and doing His will and the things, he purposes for us is what we should be striving towards; then the good things will follow (Matthew 6:33)

5.   *Pain can bring you gain when you discover, develop, and deliver His purpose for your life.* There is a process to turning pain into purpose. In that process, we may learn painful life lessons where we, and others, gain wisdom and opportunities that will push us into His purpose for our lives. Therefore, we must trust the process, because God is good, and He desires good things for us (Proverbs 3:5-6; Jeremiah 29:11).

6.   *Purpose will preserve you no matter how much pain you experience in your trials.* God will not allow more to happen in our lives than we can bear; I believe that. If God allows it, He can also use it to promote you and provide a way through it where His glory will be revealed, and it will benefit others (1 Corinthians 10:13)

7.   *Pain that pushes you into purpose will also push you into your passion and superpower.* Nothing is wasted in our lives. God uses everything to paint the canvas that reveals the masterpiece that you are (Ephesians 2:9-10; Hebrews 13:8)

8.   *Pain doesn't happen against you but for you when you bump into His Purpose for your Life.* We must repurpose our pain and leverage it by finding God's consolation so we can comfort others with that same comfort (2 Corinthians 1:3-7)

9. *When you have been impacted by extreme painful situations, your life becomes an extreme positive impact on other people's lives.* Be the salt, the influence and God will work things together for your good (Romans 8:28)

10. *Purpose will push pain back by giving you authority in a place of your calling, becoming a voice for the voiceless, and attracting an abundance of resources that will send you into the overflow that God has destined for your life.* If you are patient in the process and work diligently with what's in your hand, eventually the pain to purpose process will promote you and take you to your "promised land" in life. A land flowing with blessings (Exodus 6:8).

I pray that through my life story and the pain of incarceration you have begun to gain insight into the possibilities for your own life. You can live a life of significance by listening and obeying God, by forgiving others, serving a certain people group, creating things to help change the narrative, and believing that, like Oral Roberts would always say, "God is gooood!" (Response: "All the time"); "and all the time (Response: 'God is good)" and "Something gooood is going to happen to you today!" God is truly good all the time and I believe that God is going to do something good in your life by giving you purpose for your pain.

LIFE STORY TIMELINE

1975

Became a Drug Dealer

1980

Became Born Again Christian

1992

Received 1st Degree in Business Information Systems from

The University of Houston

1995

Attended Oral Roberts University (ORU) in their Master

of Divinity Program on a partial Scholarship

Meets Future wife Kim Robbins at ORU

Started Robbins and Associates Accounting Firm 1996

Married to Kim Robbins 1997

Graduate from Oral Roberts University (ORU) with their

Master of Divinity

1998

My Wife and I moved to Georgia and bought our 1st

Home Expands Robbins and Associates to 5 different

Cities, including Buford, GA

Our 1st Child, Janae (daughter), is born

1999

Start my first church called Crossroads International Center

2000

Our 2nd Child, Jordan (son), is born 120

2002

Closed Robbins and Associates to focus on my pastoral

ministry

Robbins and Associates Company was placed under

investigation for Tax Fraud by IRS

2003

Our 3rd child, Judah (son), is born

My former employee was indicted for 65 counts of Filing

False Tax Returns

2004

Indicted for 15 counts of Conspiracy and Filing False Tax

Returns with my former employee

Started preparing to go to trial to prove my innocence of

fomentation (formal accusation)

2005

Go to Trial to prove my innocence

Found guilty (with the help of being railroaded) on 5 counts

of Filing False Tax Returns, but Co-defendant was found

innocent of all 65 charges against him

Sentenced to 3 1/2 years in prison, to be served in Georgia

where my family and I lived

2006

Resigned from my pastoral ministry to go prison to serve

3 1/2 years in an Atlanta Federal Prison Camp in Georgia

Self-surrender into the Atlanta Federal Prison Camp in

Georgia

Appealed my conviction; however, the courts refused to answer my appeal until the last day of my sentence 2007

Overcame my bitterness and anger for God, my co-defendant, ex-lawyer, Prosecutors, and Judge

Accepted that God wanted me to do prison time to use my prison experience as a pulpit to help others

121

2008

Received six months of early release from the Second Chance Act because of good behavior. I was under house arrest

2009

Launch 2nd Church called Kingdom Life Church

Launch Life Empowerment Enterprises (LEE) Inc. -a Life Coach certification company.

2010

Volunteer to work for Prison Fellowship and return to the prison to preach

2013

Open 1st Reentry Home 2014

Launched 3rd and final Church called The Source Church 2016

Worked at the State of Georgia for the Department of

Community Supervision (DCS) (aka Probation and Parole) as

a Community Coordinator

Started Uplift (Uber Plus Lyft), 1st Reentry

Transportation service for Returning Citizens to get b

work, court, classes, and Probation Office meetings 2019

Received America Probation and Parole "Spotlight" Recipient

award for reentry innovations

Resigned from the State of Georgia DCS Job to start Safe

Staffing company right before the pandemic of 2020

2020

Founded Tackle the Shackles National Reentry Coalition 122

2021

Released my firstweekout.com documentary

2023

Opened another Reentry House from a Victory Church Christmas Gift to the World gift. We purchased a new home for formerly incarcerated individuals after being displaced from renting a home because the landlord did not want to rent to Vital Signs because they wanted to make more money with safer tenants

ABOUT THE AUTHOR

Lee Robbins is a National Reentry expert and Founder/CEO of Life Empowerment Enterprises, Inc. (**www.leerobbins.com**), a Life Coaching and Certification company. Lee has served as the Greater Gwinnett Reentry (**www.gwinnetreentry.org**) President, for which he is a perpetual volunteer connecting Partners, Providers, and Participants to reduce prison recidivism.

Lee is the former Community Coordinator for the Department of Community Supervision (**www.dcs.georgia.gov**) and is committed to building networks of resources such as housing, jobs, transportation, education, food, etc. (**www.vitalsignsreentryministry.org**) to help Returning Citizens not only have a second chance, but a better chance to succeed in life. Lee's current focus is on a new reentry 3-tier staffing company named Safe Staffing (**www.safestaffinginc.com**) to empower Returning

Citizens to obtain jobs, develop careers through obtaining certifications, and, for some, become entrepreneurs under designated apprenticeship programs.

Lee is the Founder and President of the award winning U.P.(Uber Plus) LIFT Transportation Services (www.uplifts.org) which is one of the first reentry transportation services help Returning Citizens to get to their probation office, accountability courts and special reintegration classes. He was one of three American Probation and Parole Association's (APPA) 2019 Spotlight Award winners. He also was highlighted in Iron Light's award-winning documentary called First Week Out (**www.firstweekout.com**)

Lee has a Business Computer Information Systems bachelor's degree from the University of Houston and a Master of Divinity Degree from Oral Roberts University. He has been married to his college sweetheart, Kim for over 27 years and they have 3 young adult children: Janae, Jordan, and Judah.

LET'S CONNECT

Life Empowerment Enterprises, Inc.
www.leerobbins.com

Vital Signs Reentry Housing
www.vitalsignsministry.org

Tackle the Shackles
Tackletheshackles.org
Monday Night Podcast:
https://www.youtube.com/@bettersecondchances

The Source Church www.thesource.church

First Week Out Documentary
www.firstweekout.com

UpLift Transportation Services
www.uplifts.org

S.A.F.E. Staffing
www.safestaffinginc.com

Kim Robbins Ministries
www.kimrobbins.org
@ Kim Robbins (on YouTube)